Rugger fan

- "There is only one happiness in life, to beat people up without getting arrested!"
- "Pain heals, Chicks dig scars and glory lasts forever!"
- "Rugby players are like lava lamps: good to look at but not very bright"
- "Rugby is like war; easy to start, difficult to stop...and impossible to forget"
- "The shortest word for me is I, the sweetest word for me is LOVE, but the only word for me is Rugby"
- "If you can't take a punch, you should play table tennis"

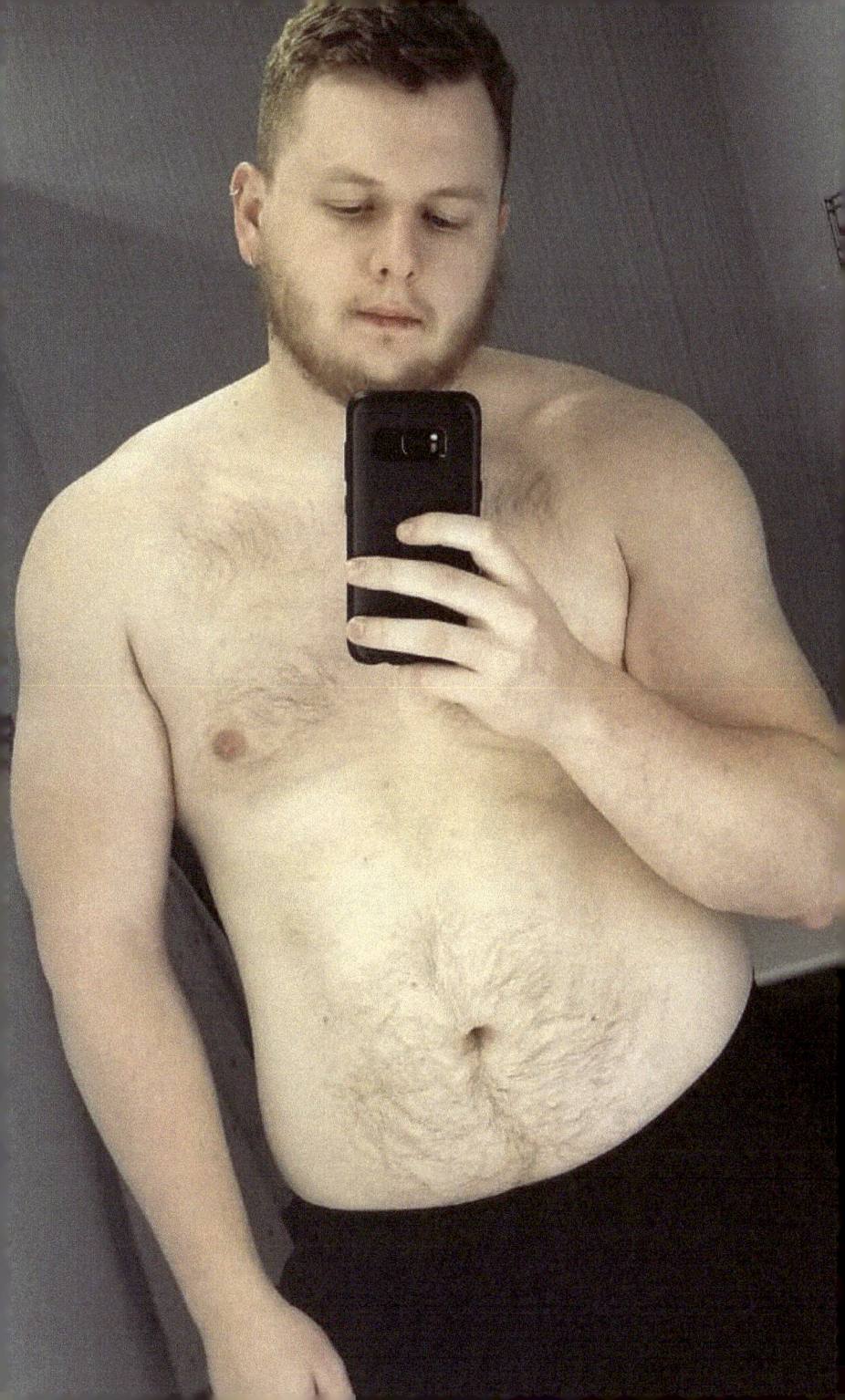

©2018 Marc Head/Jess Bunsh

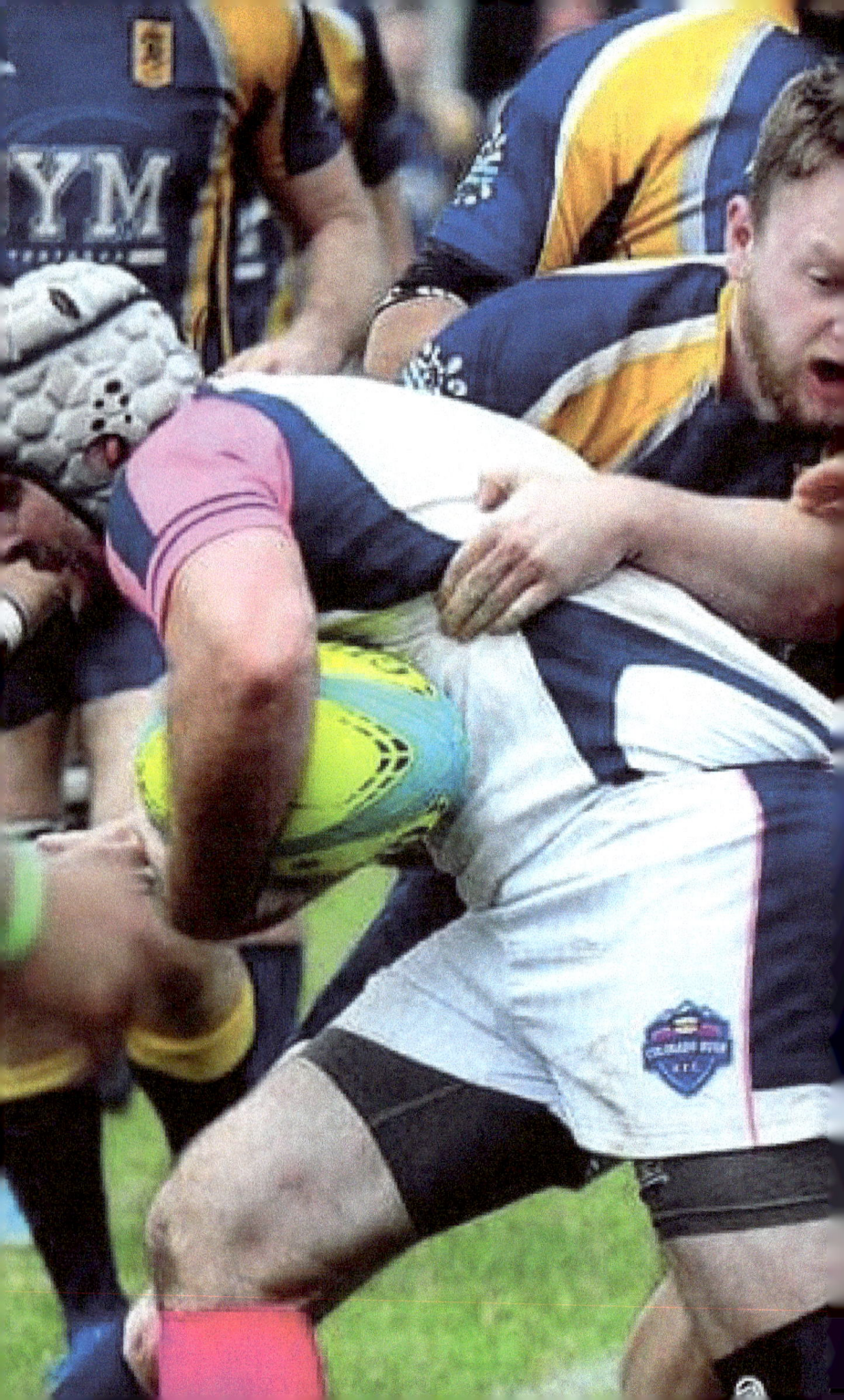

HORNET

CPSIA information can be obtained
at www.ICGtesting.com
Printed in the USA
BVHW062216120819
555663BV00022B/2024/P

9 780464 110279